IN THE MIRROR OF TIME

S. Kauser

For the old souls,
a one shot at nostalgia

S. Kauser

~MIRROR

I see me
The reflection of who I used to be
All the phases I went through
Through the ages- I grew
Oh, how the time flew

ONE

Eyes opened to a world anew
Murmurs, things, everything a blur
Only able to make visible a few
Of those surroundings, it's all a stir

TWO

My arms, my legs go up & down
I can move a bit around...
So many colours and people there can be
But only in parent's arms there is safety

MOVEMENT

Testing out
One more, two
It's a weird feeling
But I can make a few

THREE

Running through the field carefree
Led on by my curiosity
The world is a big playground
Open for discovery

FOUR

It's fun to play and talk
New toys and friends in some place called 'School'
Learning the colours and dinosaur names
Adds more to the games

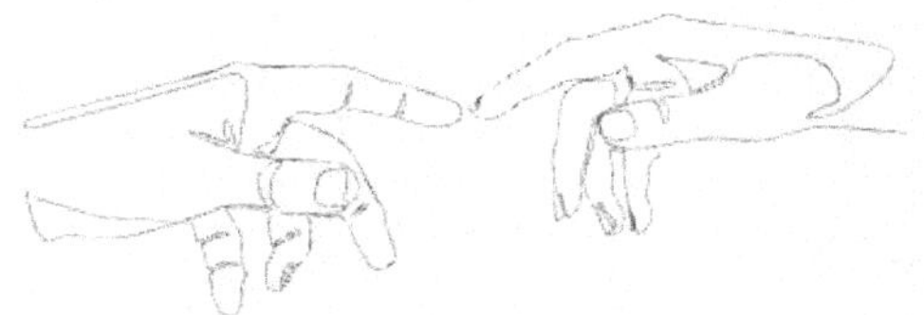

SELF-RECOGNIZE

Who is that I see
It's in the glass, in the water,
It acts the same way I do, same like I do
Wait, can it be me?

FIVE

There are dragons flying above me
Magical creatures as far as I can see
I'm called a 'funny little creature'
But I only wondered why too much

SIX

Trying new things is so much fun
But there are rules of how they're run
Been having to practice saying 'no'
The difference between right & wrong
Keeping within those lines among

KAUSERSHAKEEL

QUICK-LEARNERS

Fast to repeat, rapid to speak
Nimble as can be
I hear new words
How does the sound come from me?

SEVEN

Books with pictures are funner to read
Cars with maps racing across the pages
Rushing to figure out the adventure quest
For the beloved freezies hidden beyond

EIGHT

Science can be so fascinating
From building structures to making slime
An artistic time
Inventions I make to fight crime like the Ninja Turtles

CURIOUS

The world is so big and vast
I could sit all day and wonder quite how
The sky alone travels eons ahead
The clouds on a constant journey

NINE

My creativity stretches beyond me
Rolling forward, faster like a soccer ball
I want to be good at it all
Burst out of my little bubble and go far

TEN

What should I be when I grow up?
Dreams of what I could be so many
So many choices I find
In a circle my thoughts go-
From one idea to the next
All leading back to me
the Circle of Life as it goes

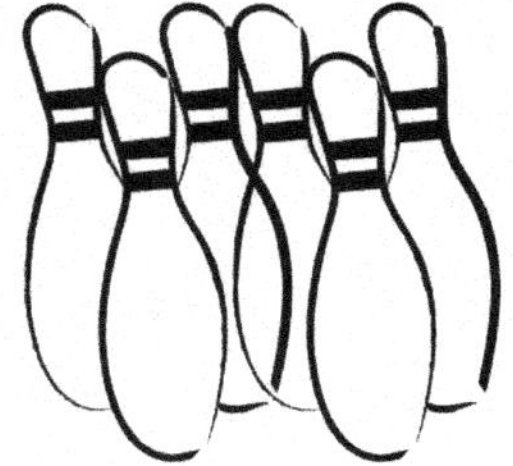

FRIENDS

We play so many games
Within our little gang
We're the coolest of the school-
main characters of the story
No one can convince us otherwise

ELEVEN

What we thought 1 + 1 equaled to
Being swag is the new norm
Changing classes, changed people
Leading to old and new feelings

TWELVE

Munching on snacks
But somehow, I'm always at edge
Too sleepy, my mood unfocused
The whispers in my head don't help

PEER PRESSURE

Voices coming in from all sides
In my head and all around
Why can't I decide
Which is right which is the jibe

THIRTEEN

Everyone looks thinner than me
Skin so much nicer
While I'm still struggling to hold my temper
Its 'attitude' now, speaking through my teeth
At least I'm a teen now, how worse can it be

FOURTEEN

High school,the place of peering eyes
Not to mention the homework load is insane
Navigating it all, what a pain
These skeptical glances push me away

HATE BEING TOLD WHAT TO DO

Irksome in a way I can barely explain
Just leave me alone
I don't want to wanna listen anyway

FIFTEEN

The dumbest ideas are the coolest
Done on impulse, so what if often questionable
We're acting like fools but still acting cool
What is the worst anyone could do?

SIXTEEN

The surrounding world is confusing
Taxes? Laws? That stuff is not taught in schools
It's stressing to think that even with all this studying
It's not going to make any more sense than it did before

Why Why Why Why Why

CONFUSED

I see things a bit differently now
Considering them more,
Even my actions are measured
The need to know 'why' more evident than ever
Reasons, explanations in detail is what I want
For it all to make sense, eventually, solace

SEVENTEEN

My future looms in front of me,
the pressure of choices and decisions
Overwhelming all these transitions
The cycle of life comes round again
teenage is more trouble than it's worth
Isn't as much fun as it seemed

EIGHTEEN

Society calls me an adult
All I feel is anxious of the 'responsibility' as a result
The freedom of adulthood is overhyped
It really does feel like real life has become

COFFEE

My parents' favourite drink
That needed boost in the morning
Never thought I'd become a contender too
In the wait in line for that morning brew
The caffeine pumping through my veins, to my brain

NINETEEN

With the increased hustle and bustle
I've learned a thing or two:
It's all a hectic whirlwind
Gotta be lively and spontaneous in the moments
It can be a struggle, caught up in the supposed "knowing what to do"
The atmosphere will either make or break you.

TWENTY

The second decade brings much insight
Only live this age once
Maturity is realizing that
you don't need to have it all figured out
There's no exact route that is wrong or right
I must prioritize myself above all
The Circle of Life in full circle
with me at the center....

ACKNOWLEDGEMENT

Special thanks to my family with whom I made these cherished memories and the lessons Iearned that will stay with me forever.

To my friends for being so supportive and encouraging through the writing process.

Am especially grateful to my wonderful beta readers team who helped me throughly edit and structure my poems to make them as perfect as this could be.

And thankyou to my personally hired cover designer, my lovely sister Safa who assisted me with the visual symbolism throughout this book.

ABOUT THE AUTHOR

S. Kauser

S. Kauser writes under the pen name 'Casey'
She is a self-published author, and enjoys working on many different forms of writings such as short stories, poems and articles.
'In the Mirror of Time' is the first book by S. Kauser.
She lives in Toronto, Ontario and attends the University of Toronto.

Follow her on:
Instagram: @casey_thewriter
Substack: @Casey's Substack
Medium

www.ingramcontent.com/pod-product-compliance
Lightning Source LLC
LaVergne TN
LVHW010123170826
845678LV00012B/2561

9781069024305